Spring

Library of Congress Number: 80-25093

1 2 3 4 5 6 7 8 9 0 85 84 83 82 81

Printed in the United States of America.

Library of Congress Cataloging in Publication Data

Allington, Richard L
  Spring.

  (Beginning to learn about)
  SUMMARY: Text, pictures, and related activities
introduce experiences traditionally associated with
spring: sports, weather, clothes, colors, feelings,
and things to see, smell, touch, and hear.
  1. Spring — Juvenile literature. [1. Spring]
I. Krull, Kathleen, joint author. II. Uhde,
Lynn. III. Title. IV. Series.
QB631.A388   500   80-25093
ISBN 0-8172-1342-2

Richard L. Allington is Associate Professor, Department of Reading,
State University of New York at Albany.
Kathleen Krull is the author of twenty-five books for children.

BEGINNING TO LEARN ABOUT

SPRING

BY RICHARD L. ALLINGTON, PH.D., · AND KATHLEEN KRULL
ILLUSTRATED BY LYNN UHDE

Raintree Childrens Books • Milwaukee • Toronto • Melbourne • London

There are four seasons in a year.

spring

summer

autumn

winter

Each season lasts about three months.
Spring is the season when nature
comes back to life after the long winter.

Spring comes after winter.
Summer comes after spring.
Which picture shows spring?

I see things that tell me spring is coming.
The days are longer and warmer. The
snow melts away. The trees grow buds.

What signs tell *you* that spring is coming?

Where I live, spring is a time
of rain and mist.

What kind of weather do *you*
have in spring?

Spring brings special feelings. I am
happy that I can spend more time
outdoors. I feel excited by all the
changes I see in nature.

What feelings do you have in spring?

I hear the sounds of spring.
Birds chirp. Grass whispers.
Water splashes in the river.

What sounds do you hear
during spring?

Spring brings special smells. I smell the
flowers and the wet earth.

What things do you smell during spring?

As the weather gets warmer, I wear lighter jackets, especially waterproof jackets.

What special clothes do you wear
in spring? Why?

Spring is a good time for
playing soccer.

What other spring sports
can you think of?

In the spring, my family has fun doing
the spring-cleaning together. I love to
help plant the garden too.

What do you like to do in spring?

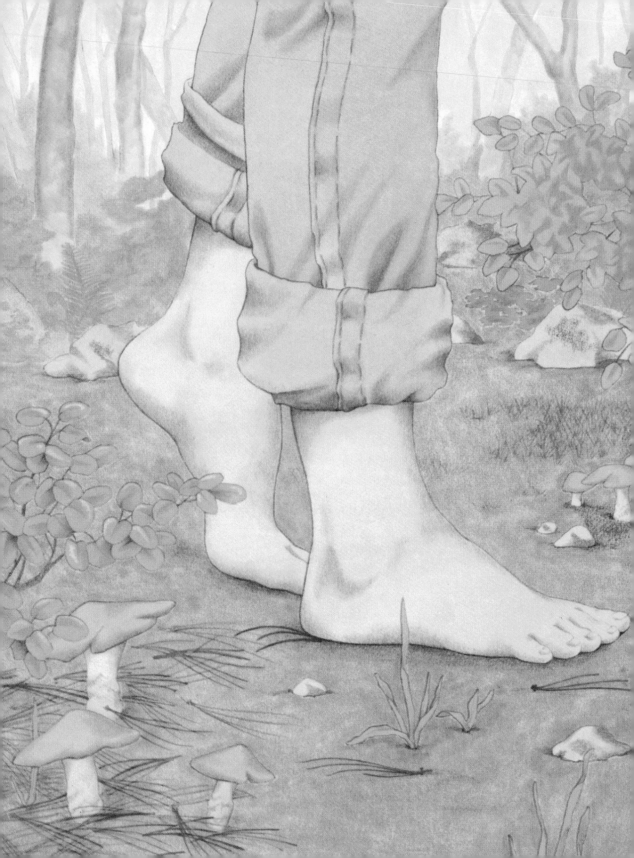

In spring I sometimes go
barefoot. My feet feel the
squishy mud and the
wet grass.

When you go barefoot, what
special things do your feet
feel in spring?

Where I live, I see more dogs and cats
in the spring. The fish are jumping.
Rabbits visit the gardens.

What animals do you see in spring?

Sometimes I get tired of
the spring rains. I wish
that school would end
and summer would start.

Are there things you don't
like about spring?

I see things that tell me spring is ending.
The days get even longer and warmer.
The grass is thicker. The trees are fuller.
I can tell that summer is coming.

What signs tell you that spring is ending?

Say the names of the twelve months in the year.
Which months are the spring months?

January	July
February	August
March	September
April	October
May	November
June	December

Make a poster about spring.
Look at a newspaper or a magazine.
Try to find pictures that remind you of spring:

things you see, hear,
taste, smell, or touch

things to do

holidays

things you like or
don't like about spring

Cut out the pictures. Tape or paste them
onto a large piece of paper or cardboard.
You may ask an adult to help you.